VOLCANOES
Journey to the Crater's Edge

Endpapers:
Furnace Peak, Réunion Island

Design Coordinator, English-language edition: Sonia Chaghatzbanian

Library of Congress Cataloging-in-Publication Data

Bourseiller, Philippe.
[Volcans racontés aux enfants. English]
Volcanoes: Journey to the Crater's Edge / Philippe Bourseiller; text by Helene
Montardre; drawings by David Giraudon; adapted by Robert Burleigh.
p. cm.
Summary: Over thirty photographs and accompanying text reveal the facts
about the world's volcanoes.
ISBN 0-8109-4590-8
1. Volcanoes—Juvenile literature. [1. Volcanoes.] I. Montardre,
Helene. II. Giraudon, David, ill. III. Burleigh, Robert. IV. Title.

QE521.3.B68513 2003
551.21—dc21
2003000971

Printed and bound in Belgium
10 9 8 7 6 5 4 3 2 1

![Abrams logo]

Harry N. Abrams, Inc.
100 Fifth Avenue
New York, N.Y. 10011
www.abramsbooks.com

Abrams is a subsidiary of
LA MARTINIÈRE
G R O U P E

VOLCANOES
Journey to the Crater's Edge

photographs by
PHILIPPE BOURSEILLER

Adapted by
Robert Burleigh

Text by
Hélène Montardre

Drawings by
David Giraudon

HARRY N. ABRAMS, INC., PUBLISHERS

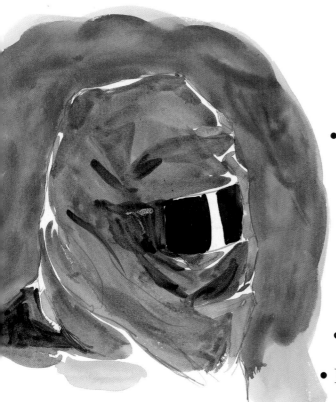

Contents

*In each photograph, a red dot on the world map marks the country
  being described.*

How are volcanoes born?

Think of this: The Earth is like a huge orange wrapped up in several "skins." First, the Earth's crust; then, the mantle; and finally, the heart, or core, where the hottest temperature burns. In fact, the farther you travel toward the center of the Earth, the higher the temperatures.

Our planet's structure

Each of these three skins is distinct from the others. The **Earth's crust** is very thin. Its outer part is cold — fortunately, because that's where we live!

The **mantle** is thick — so thick that it's usually thought of as having two parts. The part that touches the Earth's crust is called the "upper mantle." When this outer part of the mantle is mentioned along with the crust, the two are called the **lithosphere**. The inner section of the mantle is called the "lower mantle."

The Earth's **core** also consists of two parts: the outer, liquid core, and the inner, solid core.

The plates

The lithosphere is cut up into several large pieces, known as lithospheric plates. There are two kinds of plates: the continental plates, on which the continents rest, and the oceanic plates, which form the floors of the oceans.

Furthermore, these plates move — but very gradually. This is what's called plate tectonics, or continental drift. Most volcanoes on our planet form where the plates touch each other. And when that happens, a number of phenomena can occur.

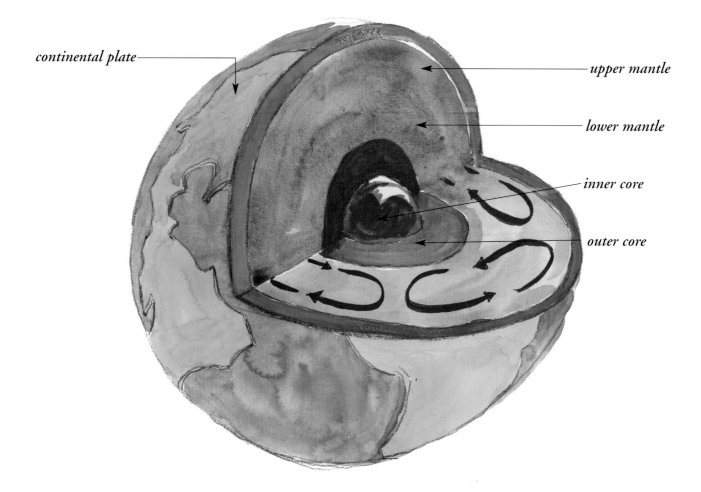

continental plate

upper mantle

lower mantle

inner core

outer core

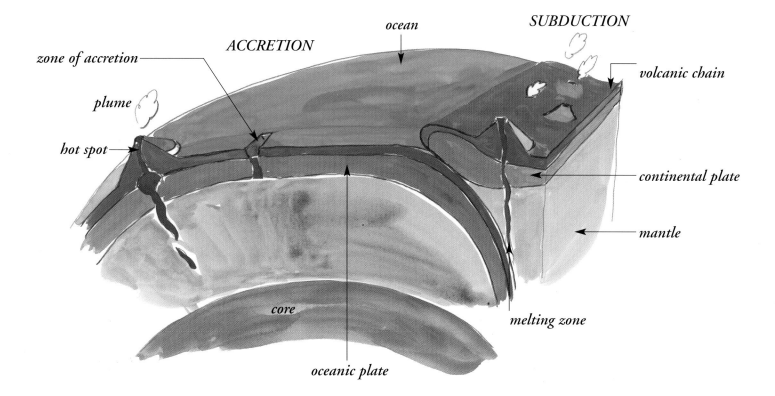

When two plates meet, one may travel underneath the other. This is called **subduction**. The explosive types of volcanoes—**gray volcanoes** — form in this way. Subduction zones account for only 15 % of the planet's volcanic activity, but these eruptions are the most spectacular, because they take place on land expelled from inside the Earth.

On the other hand, when plates move apart, the material in the Earth's lower mantle rises and "plugs" the space that has been created. This phenomenon is called **accretion.** It is how **red volcanoes**, volcanoes that spew lava, are born. The accretion zones are located on the ocean floors. They account for the greatest part of the Earth's volcanic activity — activity largely invisible to us, because it takes place underwater! Sometimes a small part breaks through the water's surface and creates land. This is how Iceland formed, for example.

Finally, **hot spots** occur when a volcano appears outside the expected volcanic boundaries in the middle of a plate, directly over a heat source located deep in the Earth.

Magma

Under pressure, the rocks that make up the Earth's mantle partially melt. These molten rocks form magma, which also contains minerals and gases. When magma reaches the Earth's surface, the gases escape, and the magma then becomes lava. It is this lava that volcanoes expel.

Lava

In the accretion zones, the magma, which contains very little silica, is extremely hot and in highly liquid form. Gases escape easily and few explosions occur. The lava is red and flows easily, sometimes over a distance of many miles. We are now talking about red volcanoes.

In the subduction zones, magma contains high concentrations of silica. This magma is, accordingly, thicker and cooler, which means that gas bubbles have more trouble escaping. This is what produces explosions. The lava is made up of fine, gray ash. The gray volcanoes are the most dangerous, because their explosions are extremely violent and unpredictable. But listen to this! Over the course of its lifetime, the same volcano can change its nature, moving from a gray to a red one, and vice versa!

How photographer Philippe Bourseiller took these pictures…

Does it seem a simple, even straightforward job, taking all of these photographs of volcanoes? It's not at all! It actually took years to gather them all together! Years of work, research, patience, study, and also . . . plenty of courage! Here's the story of how these photographs came to be.

Philippe loves open spaces, and especially deserts, where the sand burns under a fearsome sun or where ice runs to a limitless horizon. One day, in 1991, he was in the Philippines when a volcano named Pinatubo erupted. *Boom!* A monstrous plume of ash soared into the sky. *Click, click!* Philippe captured it with his camera. Rivers of mud rushed down into the valleys. Ash covered villages, fields, animals, people … It was daytime, yet it was as black as night. *Click click!* Philippe photographed in the way he always does, capturing every interesting image around him: a woman under a red umbrella (that was the only thing she found to protect herself with!), a man who was trying to lead his livestock to shelter, a farmer in his fields trying to save his crops … Beginning on that day, Philippe decided to devote a part of his photographic work to volcanoes.

First he had to get organized. To learn more, he talked with volcanologists (people who study volcanoes). Now, whenever an eruption takes place, he finds out about it and is ready to leave immediately for any spot on Earth. In his home, two bags are always packed, one for conditions of extreme cold, the other for living in hot climates. When the moment comes, he has only to pick up the right one, and then, off he goes! He's on the road!

His bag holds his photographic gear, of course, and the equipment he needs to venture out onto volcanoes: a sturdy helmet, a gas mask, a red suit that can withstand acids, glacier boots with plastic shells that protect against lava, and, if he wants to get close to lava flows, a suit made of an aluminized fabric that enables him to withstand very high temperatures. And that's not all. There's camping gear, too: tent, sleeping bag, mattress, food rations, and water — since water (as you might guess) is never found at the site of an eruption! He has to carry everything with him, and Philippe's bag is often very heavy, more than 88 pounds!

Then it's adventure time. The weather is the top priority — will it be good enough for photographing? He also must calculate the risks. How far can he go? Philippe knows that red volcanoes, the ones that spew lava like those in Hawaii, are relatively easy to approach. But gray volcanoes are a different story. They can explode at any moment, so it's important to stay at a safe distance! Regardless of the volcano's color, the main thing is to look at everything, be patient, and scout out the best perch from which to photograph. Philippe works with volcanologists who are often citizens of the country and know their volcano thoroughly. He accompanies them on their expeditions. While the scientists make observations or take samples, Philippe explores the surroundings and takes his pictures.

But the story of volcanoes is not limited to eruptions alone, a fact Philippe understands well. He travels the world, meets people, listens, attends religious festivals … In fact, people have always lived beneath volcanoes, and — looking up — they have often imagined that these mountains of fire were the dwelling places of their gods.

This is also the story Philippe tells in his photos: the history both of volcanoes and of the people who live alongside them — that is, our human history.

Volcanic cone of Lakagigar

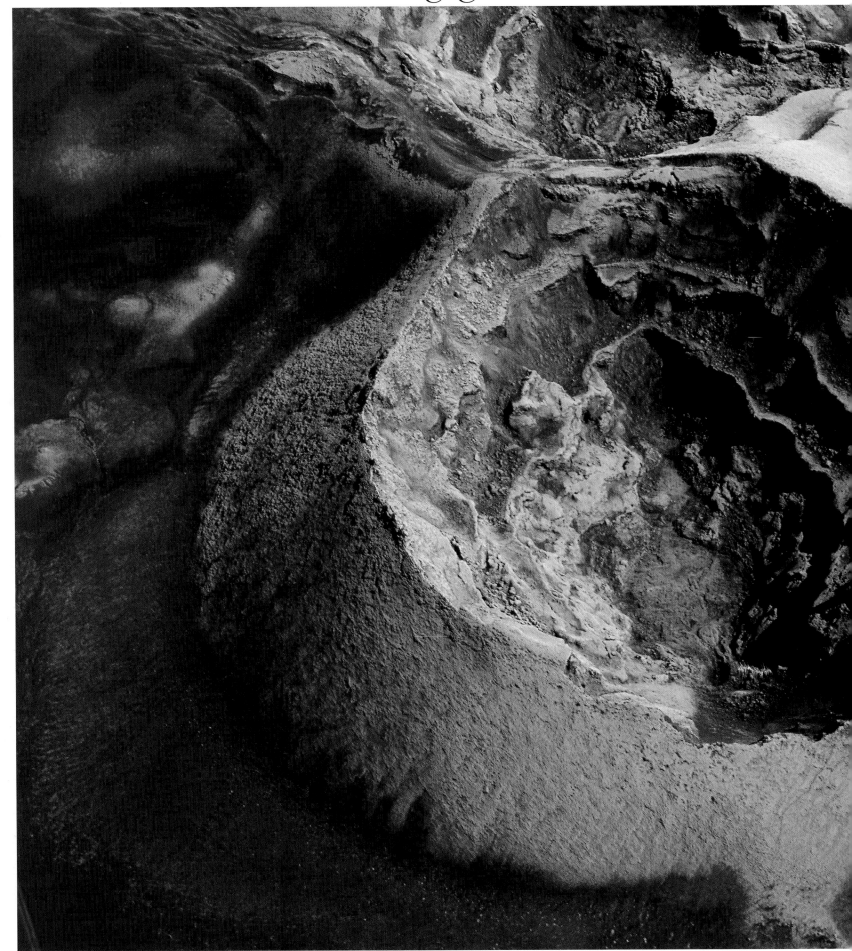

Today it is blanketed with mosses and lichens, but this volcanic cone in the Lakagigar chain is actually one of 115 craters that formed during the volcano's eruption in 1783.

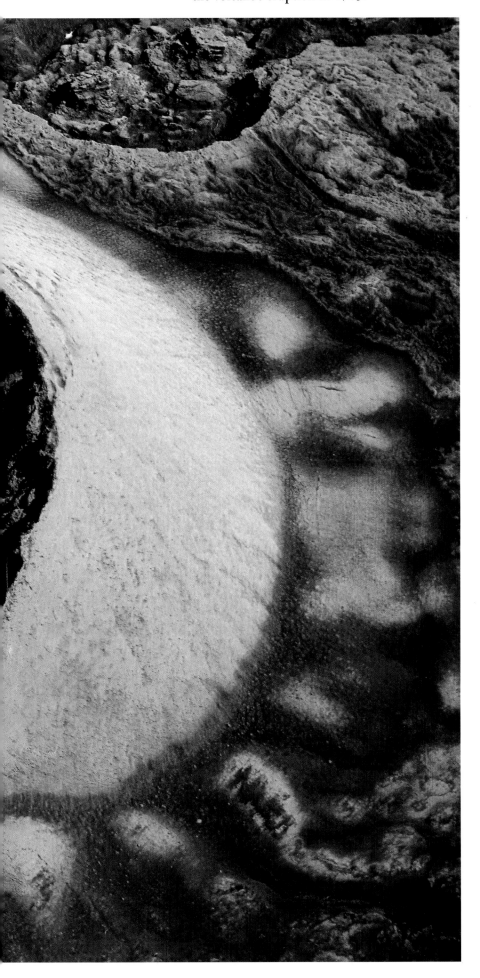

Europe

"The earth began to swell up accompanied by a chorus of howls, and inside a roaring that caused it to burst apart into fragments, rent it and ripped it open, as when an enraged animal tears something to pieces. Then flames and fire spurted from the lava . . . "

We are in Iceland in the year 1783. The author of these lines was Reverend Jon Steingrimsson. For several weeks, Steingrimsson told the story of the fantastic eruption of the Laki Volcano: 115 craters formed and blew out lava for nearly two months. Indeed, this eruption had enormous consequences for the whole Northern Hemisphere. A strange fog covered the sky. Violent storms broke out, accompanied by intense hailstorms. We now know that gases which escaped from Laki changed climatic conditions all over Europe. These gases produced acid rains that burned crops. They created a kind of "screen" between the sun and the Earth, darkening the sun. Irritant gases caused disease, crop failures led to famine, and temperatures plunged. The winters following 1783 were fearsome. And all because of one (extraordinarily powerful) volcano!

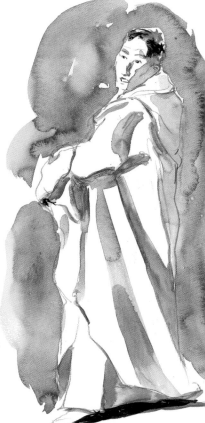

River colored by mineral salts

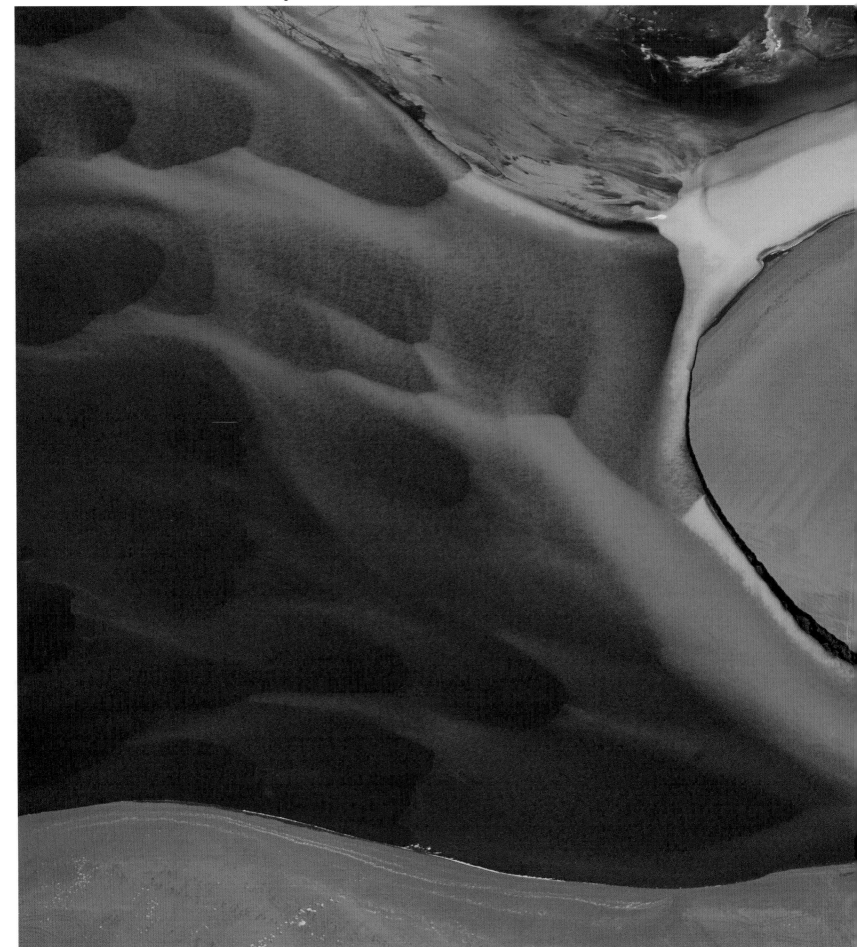

River waters draw multicolored landscapes on Iceland's surface. Seen from above, the land resembles a picture continually being repainted.

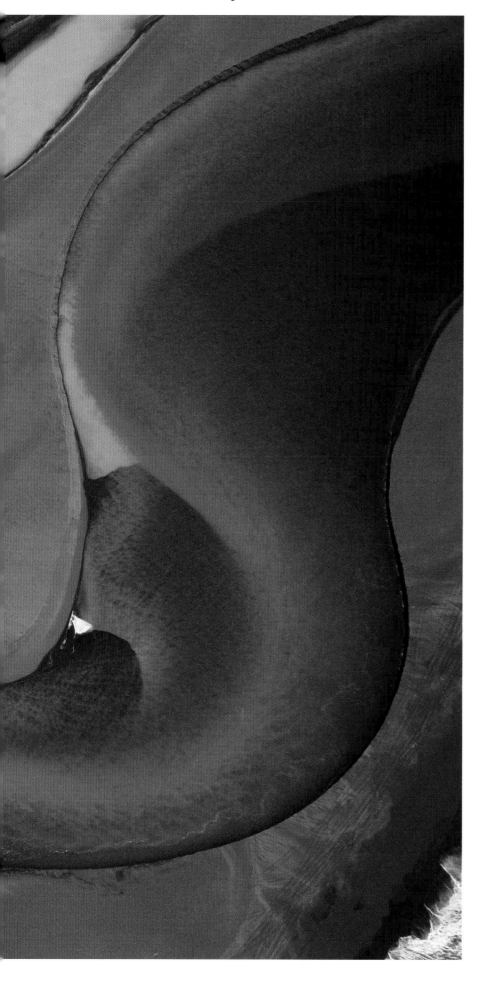

Europe

It may look like an abstract painting, but in fact it's a river. And how does it get its amazing color? Here's how.

Twenty-three million years ago, the high concentration of magma that spread over a small section of an underwater mountain chain caused the top of the chain to emerge from the sea. And so — Iceland was born! Iceland is, in fact, a volcanic island that never stops growing. Volcanic eruptions and earthquakes follow each other continually.

Today, rivers dig their paths through mineral-rich volcanic mountains. When they come into contact with volcanic rocks, they carry away mineral salts, which give the water its astonishing colors—turquoise, yellow, green, gold. Yes, the river waters in Iceland are stained with all the colors of the rainbow!

Hot spring at the base of Sakurajima Volcano

The Sakurajima Volcano counts as one of the most dangerous volcanoes in Japan. But — despite this — people have learned to live in harmony with it and to profit from its gifts, such as hot springs.

Asia

It's like a vast, protected swimming pool filled with very warm water. But it's no swimming pool at all. It's a hot spring. And Japan has many of them.

In fact, hot springs are a common attraction in the country, because Japan is a nation of volcanoes. Heat that wells up from the depths of the Earth warms the underground waters, creating the popular hot springs, where Japanese families happily go to swim.

But there's more. Heat from volcanoes also warms the sand on nearby beaches. The elderly burrow under these warm sands to relieve their rheumatism. Maybe we should call it a "sand sauna."

People have long benefited from volcanic activity. Beginning in ancient times, the Romans traveled to the hot springs near Vesuvius to treat their rheumatism or respiratory problems. And today, almost everywhere in the world, water and steam rise from the Earth, creating thermal spas that people use to help cure many diseases.

Lava lake in Ambrym Volcano

Steadied by his rope, this volcanologist begins his difficult descent. He is trying to get close to the lava lake in Benbow Crater on Ambrym Island.

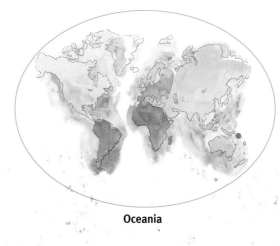

Oceania

What does it feel like, descending into a volcano's depths? Many feelings no doubt grip the volcanologist who swings over the crater floor: a slight twinge in the heart; a fear of the void; the anxiety of sensing the unstable wall start to crumble; the dread of seeing suddenly falling rocks. He feels all of this, surely, but something else, too: curiosity, the desire to learn. What will he discover at the end of his adventure?

First and foremost, the volcanologist is in search of information. He wants to learn what kind of rocks these are, what the lava that threatens to scorch him is made of, why these gases keep him from being able to breathe.

For months, he has been preparing for this moment. He must read and study the reports of those who preceded him, check his gear and measuring instruments, and, of course, obtain all of the necessary permits.

The rest is between the volcano and the person trying to understand it. While the lava boils and toxic steam dances between vertical walls, the volcanologist is concentrating. The red of his suit matches the red of the molten lava. One moment more, and he will swing closer, ever closer. Will he return safely? Who can say for sure?

Volcanologists on Merapi Volcano

These volcanologists are standing well above the clouds. As the volcano sends out gas vapor, they move forward carefully along the jagged edges of the crater.

Asia

Merapi Volcano forms one part of what is called the Pacific Ring of Fire, the greatest concentration of active volcanoes in the world. In fact, two of the plates that form the Earth's crust meet along this ring. One of the plates passes below the other, and the junction of the plates forms volcanoes.

In this photograph, two tiny silhouettes travel over the active dome of the volcano. Can you see them in the left center of the picture? Extremely high above the clouds, on a heap of rocks and ash, these volcanologists are taking samples.

People have built their houses beneath the clouds on the volcano's sides. Why? Because in this spot, the ash expelled from the volcano makes the land fertile. When it is deposited on the soil, you might say the ash is a fertilizer sent free of charge from the sky! But sometimes, burning clouds settle over the people. These are clouds of burning gas carrying lava fragments that fall rapidly down the volcano's slopes, devastating crops and villages, bringing destruction — and death.

Fortunately, volcanologists continually study Merapi. The information these scientists collect by gathering samples often enables them to warn nearby people when danger is about to descend.

Pink flamingos on the banks of Lake Bogoria

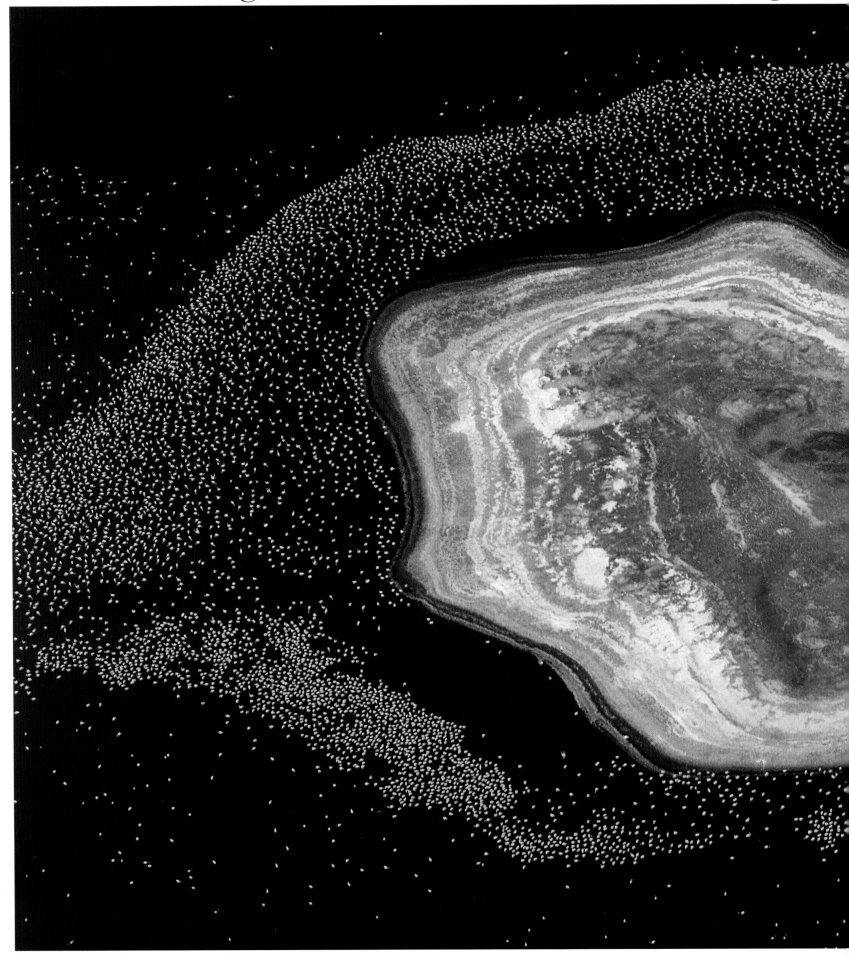

All of the pinkish-white dots you see in this picture are pink flamingos, whose unfolded wings sparkle in the sun. They come to nest in this wild place.

Africa

Can a volcano help create a lake? Yes it can, and Lake Bogoria in Kenya is one example. Lake Bogoria, one of the hottest and wildest places in Kenya, was formed by ancient volcanic activity. Today's lake actually fills what once was a volcano crater. But even though the volcano is dormant (or inactive), underground its heat remains. As a result, the lake is fed by hot springs that jet up from its depths and spread boiling water.

And that's not all. The waters from these springs are rich in mineral substances. These substances encourage the growth of microscopic algae: the food of innumerable small crustaceans. In turn, these crustaceans attract the birds that come to feed on them.

So now you know why there are so many pink flamingos on the banks of Lake Bogoria — because they can find food in abundance. And it's all thanks to an ancient volcano!

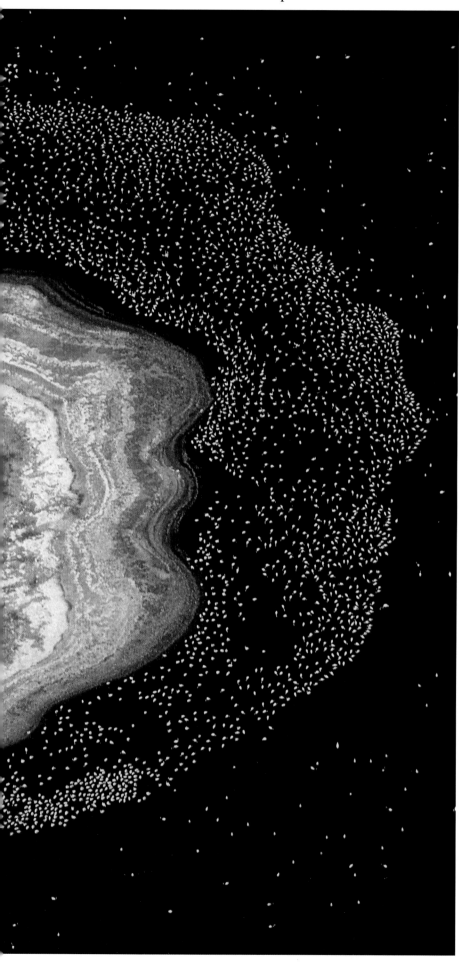

Lava lake on Erta'Alé Volcano

In a landscape from the end of time, an infernal mixture of black and glowing red boils up endlessly at the bottom of a giant cauldron. At times, it throws up sparks of fire …

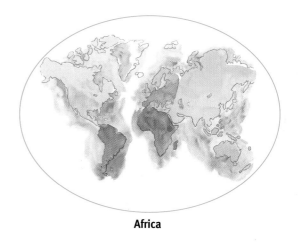

Africa

The lava lake of Erta'Alé sits on the floor of a crater nearly 300 feet deep. It is fed continually by a column of magma. The temperature of the magma remains constant, at about 1,800°F, which keeps the lava in a continuous liquid state.

A lava lake is extremely rare. If the supply of magma is interrupted, the lava will slowly become solid and the lake will disappear. On the other hand, if the magma supply increases rapidly, the lake level will rise in the crater and eventually spill over. In this case, lava flows will pour out over the volcano's sides. The lava lake thus depends on a delicate balance.

The Erta'Alé lava lake has probably been in existence for more than a century. And that's a good thing, because for volcanologists, the lake provides an extraordinary opportunity for study. This steady, persistent volcanic activity allows scientists to make measurements and analyses over long periods of time. They can decipher the signals from the volcano and match them up with volcanic activity. This information can even save lives elsewhere. The data that volcanologists gather from this single volcano formed in a far-off desert area allows them to better understand the workings of volcanoes elsewhere.

Floor of the Erta'Alé Crater

Flashes of red lightning form a zebra-like pattern over a horizon black as ink. You would think it was a stormy sky. But it is actually a lava lake …

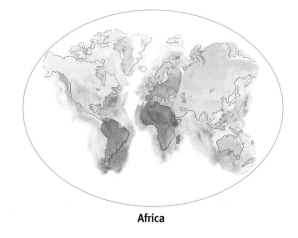

Africa

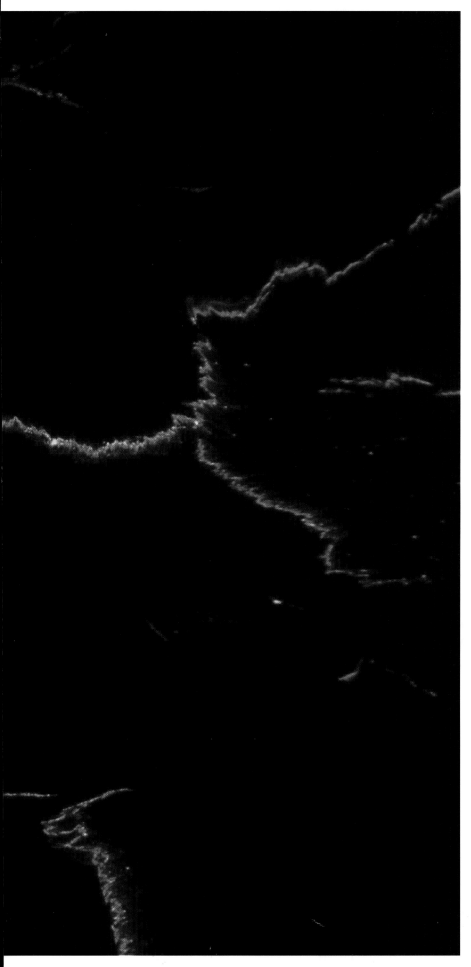

No, you are not looking up. You are really looking down — at the surface of a lake of lava.

At times, through contact with the air, the Erta'Alé lava lake cools slightly. A kind of elastic skin forms on the surface of the boiling lake, a little like the skin on hot milk when it cools, then splits up into separate sheets. The lava lake's movements are driven by currents stirred up by the agitated magma in the volcano's crater. Depending on how these currents travel, the sheets are propelled over the lake, this way and that way, back and forth.

Sometimes two sheets converge. Then several things might happen. The edge of one might pass under the edge of the other. Or else, they might collide and fold and lose their shape. But they can also slide along opposite each other. When this occurs, the lava spurts out in sparks of fire and traces in vivid red the outlines of these giant puzzle pieces. And that's what you're seeing here.

Spirit Lake ravaged by the eruption of Mount Saint H

Despite the evacuation of nearby inhabitants, the eruption of Mount Saint Helens caused about 60 human deaths. It also killed 6,500 deer and elk and 200 black bears living in the forest.

North America

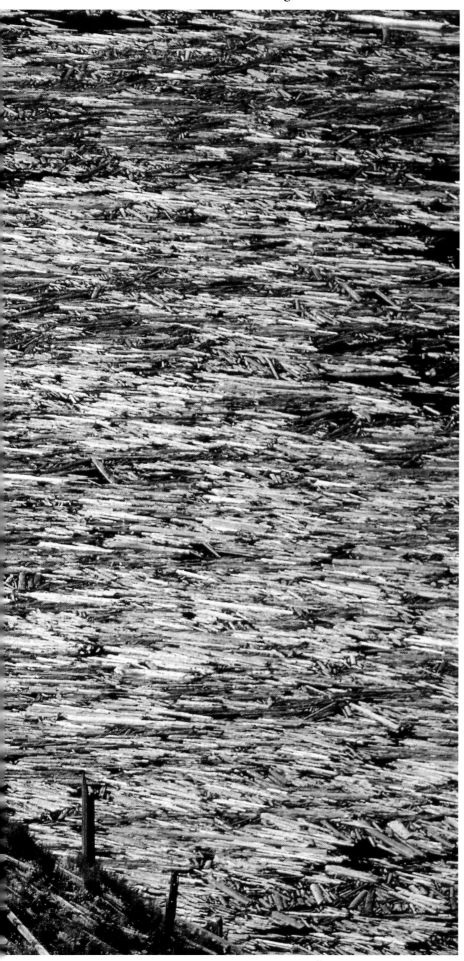

It is March 25, 1980. An earthquake signals the awakening of Mount Saint Helens, in the state of Washington. Volcanologists rush to the scene. For nearly two months, they monitor the stages leading to the tremendous eruption that is about to happen. The most visible sign is this: The volcano's summit becomes deformed and swells bigger every day. Why? A pocket of thick magma has risen from the depths and accumulated below the summit. This "lump" expands day by day.

Then, on May 18, 1980, the Earth trembles and the hump collapses, releasing an avalanche of debris that streams down the slope. *Boom! Boom*! Two explosions occur. One throws out a gigantic plume into the air. The second occurs on the volcano's side, producing a cloud that travels nearly 700 miles an hour! This enormous blast uproots all of the trees within a distance of 350 miles. Within a single minute, the lush forest of Mount Saint Helens is transformed into an arid desert where only a deathly silence reigns. Volcanoes' mysterious and terrifying power has announced itself once again.

Dromedaries crossing the Danakil Depressi

These caravans of dromedaries (the single-humped cousin of the camel) tread the soil of a vast plain that was once an ocean. High volcanic chains dominate the landscape.

Africa

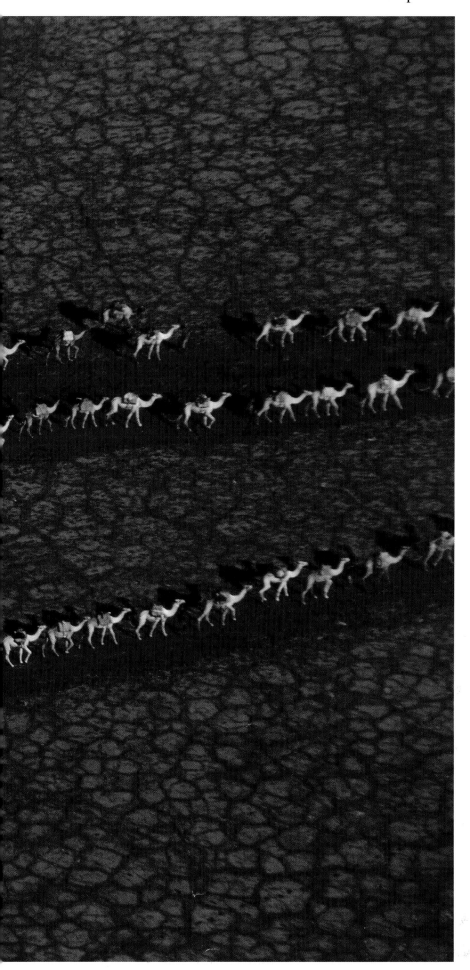

Can this dry space have once been different? Did fish or other sea creatures swim where dromedaries now plod slowly back and forth? The answer is yes!

For several million years, repeated volcanic eruptions have caused upheavals in this part of the globe. A gigantic fissure appeared, called the East African Rift.

The Danakil Depression forms one of the lowest parts of the Rift. On a number of occasions, the Red Sea flowed in and covered this area, changing it into an immense salt lake. These alternating periods of ocean flooding and evaporation deposited layers of salt, which reach a thickness of 3,000 feet in places.

Salt is essential for human nutrition and for the feeding of many animals. Merchants and their caravans of dromedaries descend from the high Ethiopian plateaus, returning loaded down with their precious salt cargo.

Eruption of Furnace Peak on Réunion Islan

Volcanoes sometimes display breathtaking fireworks. At Furnace Peak, bolts of lava are shot upward from 60 to over 1,000 feet high!

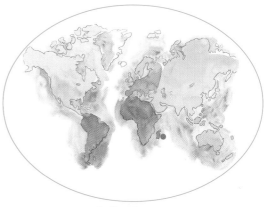

Indian Ocean

The heat is intense, beyond anything you can imagine. The glare from the bright fires could blind unprotected eyes. And yet, a man is standing there, contemplating the fantastic fireworks of the volcano. Thousands of yellow and red sparks burst forth, forming a fountain that flows down the volcano's slopes.

The man watching seems fascinated. But there is no chance he will forget what he came to accomplish. And what, exactly, is that? In a few moments, he will approach the molten lava and, using a long shovel, pull away a ribbon of it, which he will quickly pour into a metal bucket filled with distilled water. His goal is to cool the sample and solidify it as quickly as possible, so he will have congealed lava straight from the volcano.

Later, in a laboratory, scientists will saw the congealed lava into sections, then examine these sections under a microscope. Volcanologists will determine its composition and gather data about this volcano in particular, and about the changes occurring in the magma over time, in general. Little by little, scientists are uncovering the secrets of volcanoes.

Crater of the Ol Doinyo Lengaï Volcano

What a strange landscape! With its white shapes rising vertically out of the ground, you would think you were on the moon. Not at all — it's simply the crater of a rather peculiar volcano.

Africa

It is a white, tortured land where strange chimneys stand on end, their shadows lengthening under the waning sun. Nothing grows here. Yet someone has come to explore this bleak volcanic landscape. Can you find him or her? Yes, there — the tiny figure dressed in red pants in the lower right corner of the photograph. The area is so untouched that the person walks on soil still bearing the marks of the most recent eruptions!

The Ol Doinyo Lengaï volcano is extraordinary. It expels lava in a highly fluid state and at a very low temperature, between only 900° and 1,000°F (typically, lava's temperature can exceed 1,800°F). The lava is quite dark in color when it leaves the crater, but becomes white as it cools. Why? Because the magma the volcano discharges contains high concentrations of carbon dioxide and sodium carbonate. This substance, called carbonatite, whitens as it cools, giving a snowy appearance to the volcano's crater.

Mud bowls, Uzon Crater, Kamchatka

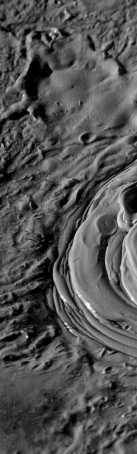

Undeniably peculiar . . . this mud of a pretty gray color boils, makes bubbles, gives off steam. But this is one mud bath you wouldn't want to jump in, because it's white-hot! It looks like a miniature volcano . . . and it is!

Asia

Volcanoes come and go, over long periods of time. And what they sometimes leave behind may surprise you. Listen to this:

A caldera is a large crater. It's what remains when the volcano summit crumbles in on itself. This can happen after an extremely strong eruption. The Uzon Caldera on Kamchatka (in Siberia) is one example. It forms a gigantic bowl with a floor lined with mud pools!

Even when a volcano becomes inactive, the subterranean, or underground, layer continues to radiate heat for thousands of years after the eruptions. At times, it's the ground that is hot; at other times, it's the underground waters, which create hot springs. At still other moments, mud bowls form. How so? The mud is heated by red-hot gases streaming up from the Earth's depths. That's why it boils continuously! These "miniature volcanoes" enable scientists to better understand how volcanoes work under real conditions.

A shelter on a road near Sakurajima Volcano

Located on the island of Kyushu in Japan's southern region, Sakurajima is in a state of virtually constant eruption. Its violent explosions shake the surrounding towns and villages.

Asia

Look out above! Something is starting to rumble and send huge columns of smoke into the air. Time to take cover — especially if you're near the Japanese volcano called Sakurajima.

Japan lies on the Pacific Ring of Fire, an area of the world containing many active volcanoes. So in this country, people are always near a volcano — which means they have to learn to live alongside their dangerous neighbors.

Fortunately, every possible measure has been taken to protect people. Along the road, shelters have been built for drivers. (Do you see the man standing there, just having left his car?) Telephone booths are covered with solid concrete slabs. People have constructed dikes in riverbeds to slow down any potential mudflows. Illuminated signs set up along the road warn drivers against falling ash that could limit visibility. Children wear helmets when they go to school. In the event of an eruption, there is only one thing to do: stop, take shelter, and don't lose your cool.

Masai tribesmen near Ol Doinyo Lengaï Volca

The volcano sometimes rumbles and spits smoke. At other times, its peak vanishes in the clouds. This may be the reason the Masai believe that a god lives there.

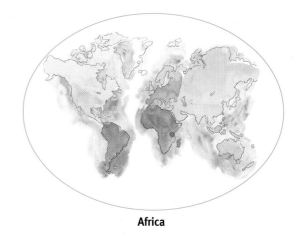

Africa

You might think people would always run from a volcano. But some people not only live near one, they use the land at its base. They even view the volcano as a god.

The Masai people are herders. They follow their flocks onto the high grassy plateaus of Tanzania. In this flat land, two things stand tall: the Masai and the massive Ol Doinyo Lengaï Volcano, profiled against the sky.

Sometimes the volcano rumbles. It spews lava and spits smoke. The ground trembles and the sky darkens. Even then, though, the Masai don't flee. They approach the volcano and allow the volcanic ash to rain down on their heads, their skin, and their flocks. For the Masai, the mountain is sacred, and the god who lives there proves that he does not forget humans by raining ash down on them. Ash is the symbol of divine water that purifies their bodies, their souls, and their hearts.

Underground ice gallery inside the Vatnajökull Glaci

It isn't heat you have to be afraid of here, but cold! You can't explore glaciers without the right equipment, including a thermal suit, boots with plastic shells, gaiters, and gloves.

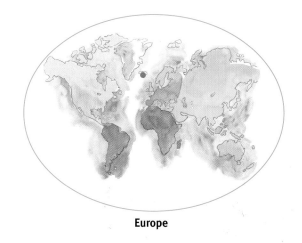

Europe

Brrrr! The man gazing at all that ice isn't in Antarctica. He's standing inside an icy cavern, sculpted by a volcano's heat, in Iceland.

Iceland is a volcanic island lying on the boundary of the Arctic Circle. But it is also covered in part by glaciers — think of the word Iceland itself! But you mustn't trust the ice, for heat gathers beneath the cold earth, and — be warned! — the volcanoes are not sleeping.

The Grimsvötn Volcano is very active. The hot steam radiating from the volcano hollows out huge galleries and tunnels in the Vatnajökull Glacier. They penetrate deep below the ice cap, to a depth of around 375 feet. You will find these only where volcanoes lie beneath glaciers, sometimes stretching out for miles underground. No wonder Iceland is often called the Land of Fire and Ice!

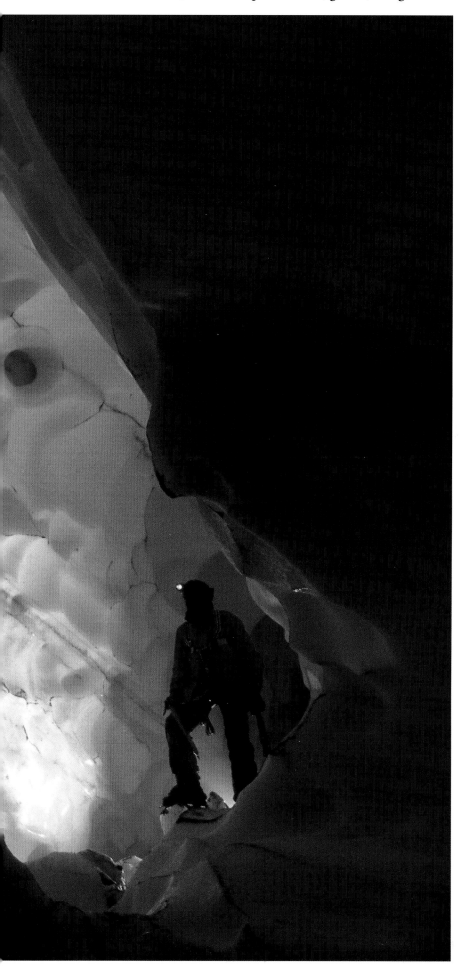

Church sculpted into volcanic deposits

The churches of Lalibela are named for King Gadla Lalibela, who wanted to build a pilgrimage site in the Ethiopian mountains.

Africa

At first glance, you may imagine this building — an ancient church — was dropped in place by a giant crane. But not at all.

They have no bricks, no mortar, no wood, and no stone, yet the churches of Lalibela are as sturdy as any buildings in the world. These churches, which number about a dozen, were sculpted into the volcanic ground between the twelfth and thirteenth centuries, almost 1,000 years ago!

Thirty million years ago, a volcanic upheaval took place here. Thousands of lava flows piled up on top of one another, reaching a thickness of nearly 10,000 feet and spreading over an area about as large as the state of Texas.

Builders sculpted the churches within these piled up lava layers, called trapps. It was no easy task, but trapp rock has one special property that aided the builders: it can be worked easily without crumbling.

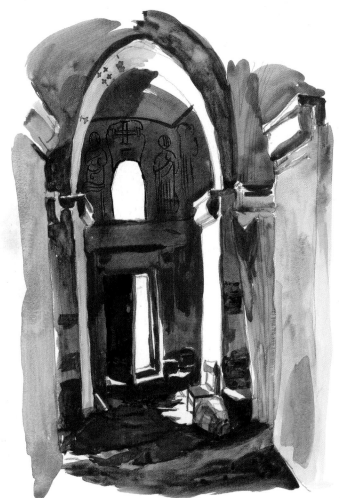

Furnace Peak, Réunion Island

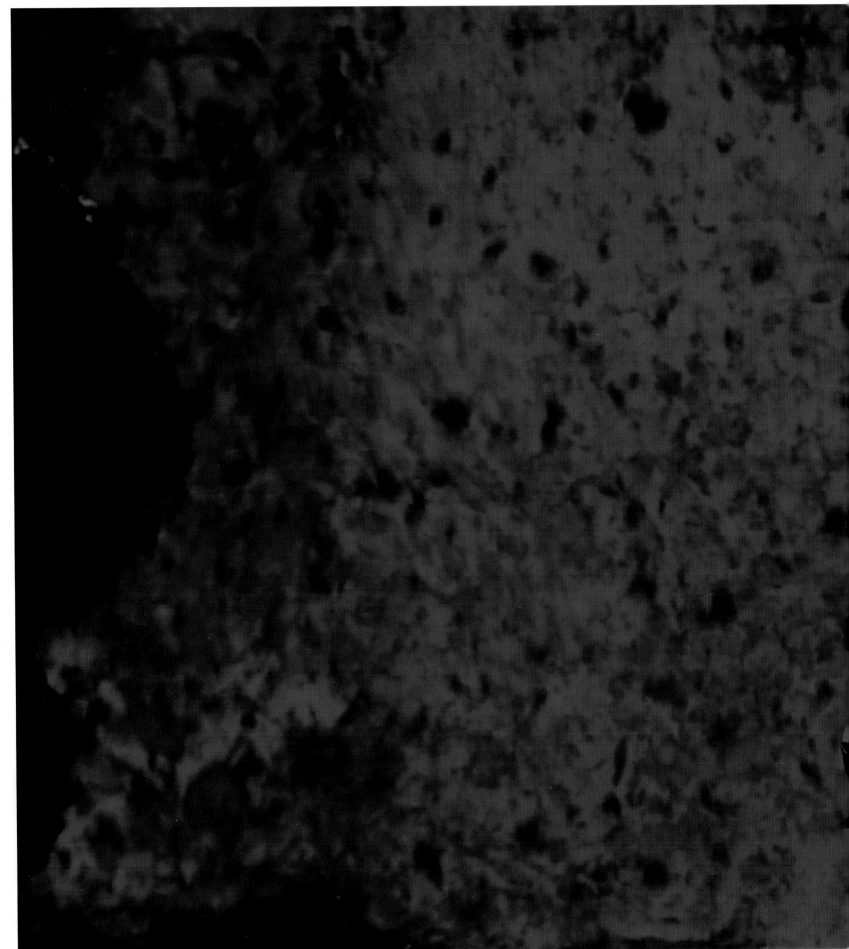

This volcanologist is not alone when he nears the molten lava. Volcanologists should always go in pairs. Each person watches to make sure that the other does not become trapped by the flowing lava.

Indian Ocean

Amazing as it seems, you can get very close to parts of an active volcano. But don't try it alone. Don't try it without the right equipment. And don't try it unless you know a great deal about volcanoes!

If you want to touch molten lava with your finger, you'd better have the right gear! Yes, you could get to within a few yards of the lava wearing long sleeves and pants. But there's a threshold you must not cross, like a burning wall beyond which you cannot take a single step.

Volcanologists use the proper equipment to cross this wall of heat. They wear a jacket and pants made of aluminized Nomex, an inflammable material that reflects the heat back, and a helmet with a wide hood. The window in the hood is made of two plates of glass surrounding a polished gold sheet that protects against the heat. On their feet they wear thick-soled boots.

Even with all this equipment, the heat still threatens. The scientist must not stay near the molten lava for more than a few seconds.

Lava flows, Kilauea Volcano, Hawaii

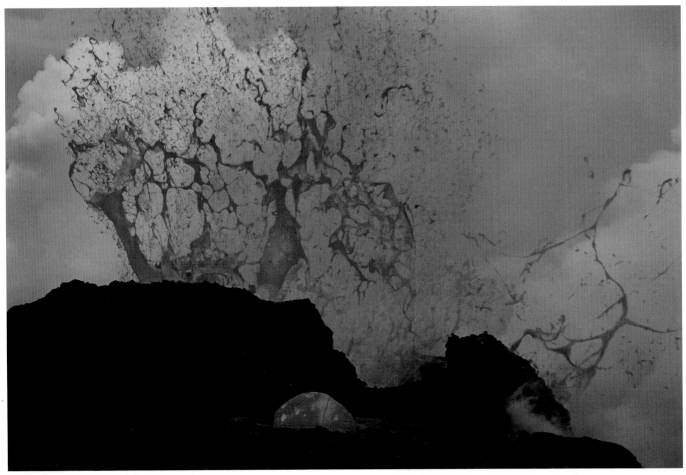

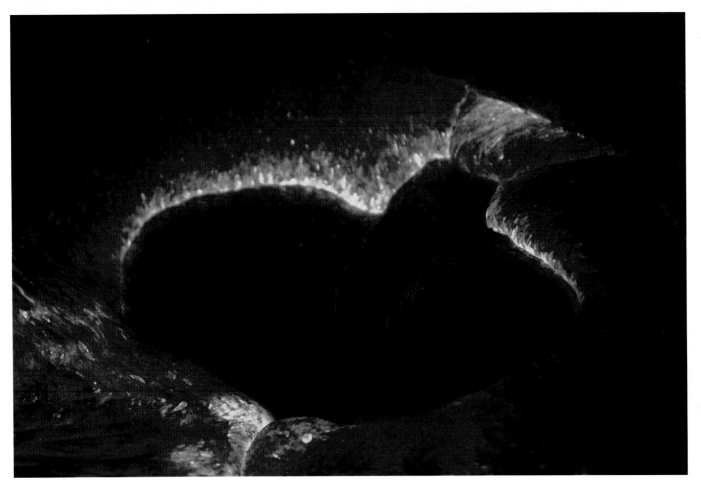

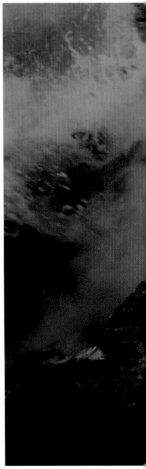

The Hawaiian word *pahoehoe* is used to describe lava flows such as the ones Kilauea emits. This lava emerges in smooth streams.

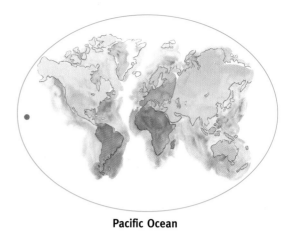

Pacific Ocean

In the photographs are remarkable examples of the different kinds of lava flows from a single Hawaiian volcano.

The lava from Kilauea Volcano flows easily, and it hardens into some odd shapes. It can form slabs, ropes, or sausage-like forms. Sometimes, it explodes noiselessly, and ribbons of lava dance in the air like fiery butterflies. (That's the photo in the upper left.) But where does all this lava go?

The lava flows down and meets the ocean at the base of Kilauea. When it comes into contact with the water, plumes of steam rise into the air. The shore seems to be on fire, and the ocean breathes smoke. Some of the lava hardens and builds up on the land, pushing the water back. Little by little, the volcano advances on the sea. Since 1983, the year in which the eruption began, the Big Island on which Kilauea sits has gradually increased its size.

Lava bubble in Kilauea Volcano, Hawaii

Magma contains gases that are released when they reach open air, creating huge lava bubbles. This one is 15 feet high.

Pacific Ocean

Is it a red creature balanced on one leg? Or is it magma? Today we have scientific explanations for volcanoes. But earlier people explained these tremendous forces by telling stories that became myths. Listen to the story of Pele and her many volcanoes that became the Hawaiian Islands.

Once upon a time there was a goddess named Pele who had a very bad temper. After a violent dispute with her sister, she was forced to run away. She settled on an island in the Pacific Ocean and started a fire. At once, her sister sprang up to chase her away. Pele moved to another island and, again, lit a fire. But her sister showed up there, too! The two goddesses pursued each other from island to island and, each time, Pele lit another fire. She finally took refuge on the Big Island on the summit of Kilauea Volcano, and her sister gave up the chase. But Pele still has her bad temper! If something rubs her the wrong way, she taps her foot on the ground, shaking the Earth and spewing out lava once again!

Summit of Cotopaxi Volcano

Cotopaxi last erupted in 1942. During the eruption of 1877, the mudflows extended about 60 miles from the volcano.

South America

Above the clouds, in an azure sky, whiteness, silence, and cold reign. From a distance, it almost looks like a beautiful metallic sculpture. But appearances can be deceiving. On the mountain peaks, beneath the snow and ice, fire is stirring lightly, waiting, waiting, waiting …

Cotopaxi Volcano in Ecuador is one of the highest active volcanoes in the world. It reaches its highest altitude at more than 19,000 feet. It sleeps now. But one day, it will awaken again.

The snowpack covering this volcano makes any eruptions even more dangerous. That's because the eruption causes tremendous volumes of ice to begin to melt. Then vast streams of mud torn from the mountain rush down the slopes and invade the valleys, drowning everything in their path. In this place more than in any other, it is extremely important to warn the inhabitants. When the eruption comes, minutes are the difference between life — and death.

Erosion near Mount Pinatubo Volcano

What a strange landscape! In the fading light, volcanologists are examining the curious shapes that have engraved themselves into the snowy-white ground.

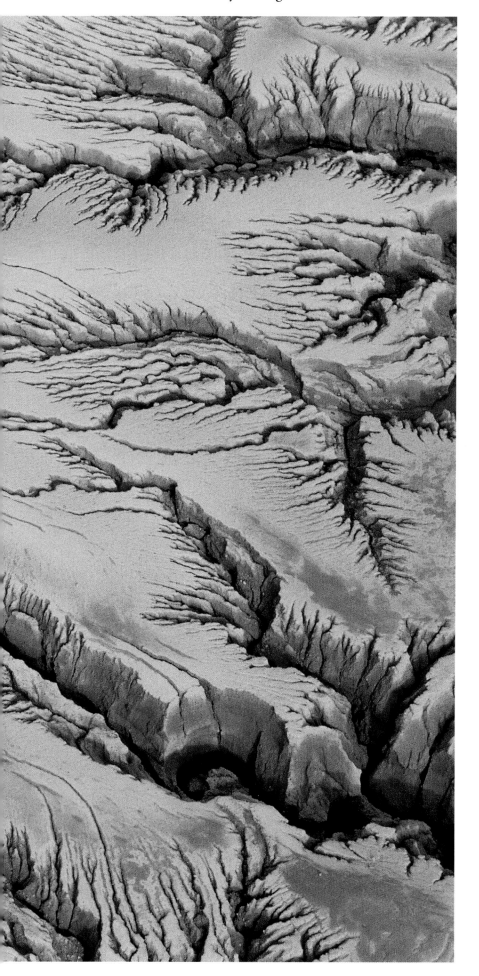

Asia

What is this? Is it a huge drawing of tree branches? Or a carving of these same branches in soft snow? Well, in fact, it's neither.

There are no trees in this place. Nor is there any snow. Instead, this twisted and tortured ground is the result of "pyroclastic flows" that rushed down the slopes of Pinatubo Volcano at the time of a 1991 eruption. And what exactly is a pyroclastic flow? Also known as a burning cloud, a pyroclastic flow is a mixture of high-temperature gases, ashes, rocks, stones, and miscellaneous debris. This mixture travels downward as fast as an avalanche, and then piles up on the ground many feet deep.

But nothing stays the same. Erosion begins its work immediately. Water, wind, and weather attack this newly deposited material and dig ravines into it. Indeed, in time, these simple fissures will become real canyons!

Evacuation drill near Sakurajima Volcano

Well protected under their helmets, the young children await orders. In Japan, children and adults are warned about the dangers of volcanoes — and each person is ready to confront them.

Asia

What do you do if you're in school — and a volcanic eruption threatens? Preparation is everything, and in this Japanese school, everyone is prepared.

The alarm sounds, and the children are already on the move. As soon as the warning siren goes off, they take shelter under their desks. Why? Because it's possible that — with no warning — the school roof will collapse! Several minutes later, the teachers give precise orders. The children stand up and quickly gather their helmets and bags in the coatroom. Next, they walk in careful formation to the main street of the town.

Skyward, helicopters swing around in search of any wounded. As the engines roar, the young schoolchildren hurry down the street to the port of Arimura, where a concrete building designed to withstand bombs and volcanic ash serves as a shelter. Soon a boat will arrive to evacuate them.

The children in the photograph look out calmly. On this day, they face no risk. It's simply a yearly drill! But on the day an eruption actually occurs, they will be ready and know how to act.

Procession along the slopes of Agung Volcano, Bali

Against the green of the rice fields, pilgrims advance toward a temple on the slopes of Agung Volcano. They wear magnificent clothing corresponding to the color of the god whom they honor.

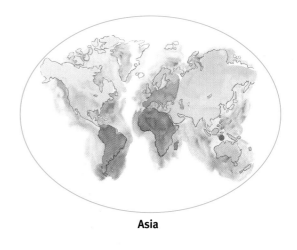

Asia

The Hindu religion honors several gods. Every ten years on the island of Bali, thousands of Hindus participate in a ceremony on the slopes of Agung Volcano. The three-day event includes prayers, offerings, and a solemn but joyful march up the side of the volcano's now-grassy slope.

Everything begins at the sea's edge. The gods are invited to house themselves in sumptuously decorated chests. Next, in a large procession, chests are carried across the entire island to the temple on the volcano's slopes. The faithful wear magnificent costumes to honor the gods. Do you see the different-colored banners? In these processions, the red banners honor Brahma, the creator; the black banners Vishnu, the protector; and the yellow and white, the destroyer Shiva and Siddhartha, the founder of Buddhism.

For the Balinese, the volcano represents the origin of the world and of life. The crater symbolizes a door opening into the world of the god Brahma. The ceremony is intended to bring all the gods together. They will then be able to change the forces of evil into forces of good, achieving a new balance in the world.

Lake Assal on the floor of the East African Rift

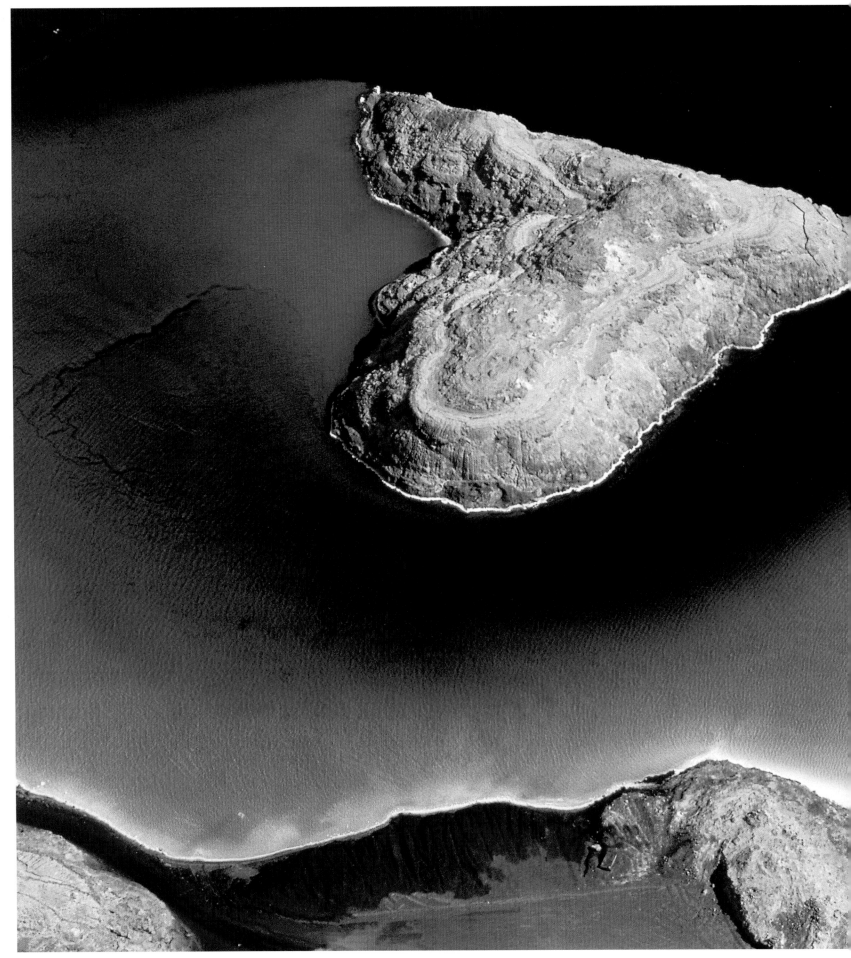

Turquoise water, islands, peninsulas, and white beaches . . . It's a dream landscape! But don't let that fool you. In Lake Assal, no life is possible, because the water is too salty!

Africa

If it were as perfect as it looks in the photograph, Lake Assal would attract vacationers from around the world. But as it is, the only visitors it attracts are scientists who want to learn more about the Earth's workings.

Lake Assal, in East Africa, is unusual. First, its surface lies nearly 500 feet below sea level. Second, its waters are extremely salty, because it is fed from salt springs. Nothing can live in such salty water.

It all began 30 million years ago. At that geologic moment, the African continent began to break open under intense underground pressures. An enormous fissure formed. It was around 2,500 miles in length and stretched across East Africa from north to south. In fact, the so-called East African Rift, of which the lake is a part, is still visible from high above. The astronauts saw it from the moon with the naked eye!

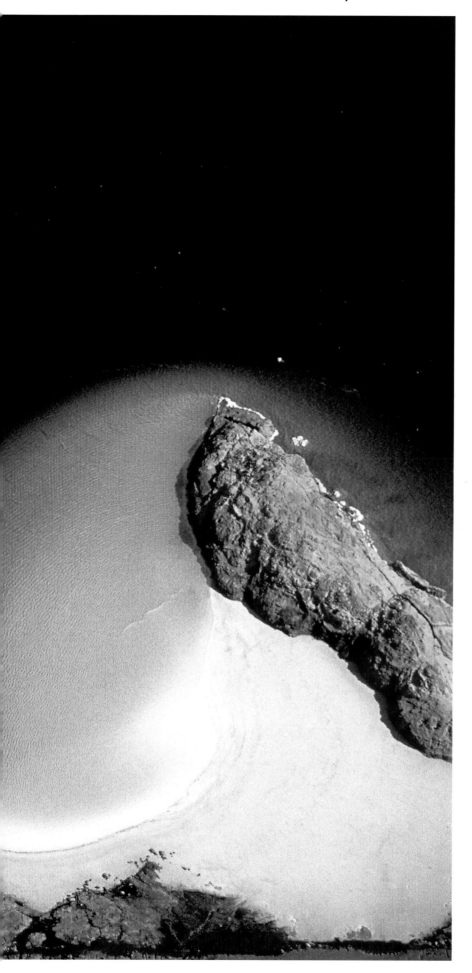

Underwater lava tunnel, Galápagos Islands

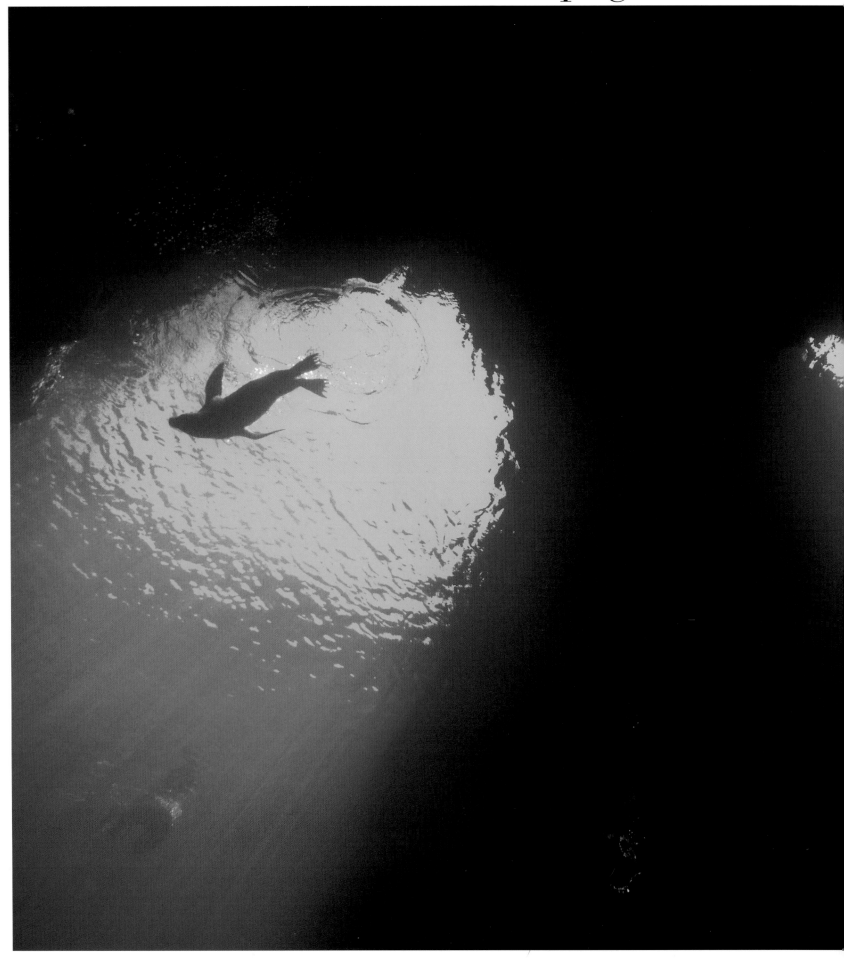

Observers should not be taken in by this enchanting landscape. In the Galápagos Islands, Nature is queen and the living conditions are harsh. It's up to the animals to adapt!

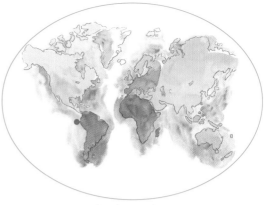

South America

Slowly and calmly, through sunlight-filtered clear water, a sea lion weaves between black rocks. But the dark tunnels through which it swims are still changing.

The Galápagos Islands are huge volcanoes that ultimately rose above the ocean. Lava piled up, century upon century, under the sea before the first islands broke the surface. Even today, a number of the volcanoes remain active. Their liquid, glowing lava rushes over the ancient flows and plunges into the ocean. The cooling lava congeals in massive black forms as it ceaselessly reshapes the outlines of the shore.

Below the waves in the marine depths, a strange and beautiful architecture is being fashioned: gigantic arches, peaceful hills, deep valleys, grottoes, and tunnels. They are all secret places of refuge for many sea creatures.

Man and his livestock during the Pinatubo eruption

Fine ash makes the air unbreathable. There is only one thing to do: leave quietly and drive one's livestock far from these places where volcanic ash blankets everything.

Asia

The strange-looking herder in the photograph is protecting himself as well as he can with a piece of fabric covering his mouth. He's trying to lead his livestock far from the ash that the erupting volcano has expelled. If his animals swallow too much ash, they will die, because the silica contained in the ash can puncture even the strongest stomach.

Volcanoes that produce explosive-type eruptions are often found in the most populated areas. But why do people live near volcanoes? It's because the accumulating ash that settles after an eruption makes a wonderful fertilizer. It mixes with the earth, forming a rich, fertile soil that farmers find useful. In these places, it is easy to grow anything.

That's why people return to their damaged or destroyed homes. The human memory is short, too. A span of just two generations is all that's needed to forget a volcanic eruption. And so life goes on under the shadow of this mountain that gives riches — and sometimes, quite suddenly, takes them away.

Ash plume during the Pinatubo eruption

Between June 12 and 15, 1991, explosion followed explosion. Ash from Pinatubo carried by the wind spread over virtually all of our planet.

Asia

Danger and darkness! A gigantic plume surges from the mountain's summit. It rises into the sky, more than 30 miles high, mixing with the clouds, and blackening the sun.

It is June 12, 1991. Pinatubo does not even appear on the list of the world's active volcanoes. For more than 600 years it has slept on, its lethal eruptions forgotten. But some volcanoes never really sleep. In April 1991, explosions had alerted volcanologists. From a study of the volcano's history, they realized that Pinatubo had triggered violent explosive eruptions in the past. And now it would do so again.

In this case, it is not the fiery lava that arouses fear, but something worse. Pinatubo belongs to the dreadful category of explosive volcanoes called gray volcanoes. Thick, viscous magma captures and holds gas bubbles, which cannot be released. The pressure builds and builds until in a single blast, the volcano expels particles of hardened lava: dust, ash, small stones, and enormous blocks thrown upward together to form this monstrous plume. But the worst is yet to come. It all falls back to Earth, completely covering a radius many miles wide. It is impossible to breathe the air. Here there is only darkness and death.

Fallout of ash expelled by Pinatubo

When Pinatubo erupted, the people living closest to the volcano were evacuated, about 300,000 in all. In this village about fifteen miles from the volcano, the villagers take advantage of a break in the ash storm to venture outside.

It looks at first like a strange combination: a black-and-white and a color photograph. But this is no photographic trick. Unfortunately, it is all too real!

Everything — houses, posts, electric wires, the leaves on the trees — everything is cocooned in a strange, gray substance. The sky is black, too, but unbelievable as it seems, it is still the middle of the day!

The ground is blanketed and the people of the village shield themselves as well as they can with umbrellas, to ward off the still-falling ash. (But one daring boy is going out for a bike ride!) The eruption of Pinatubo was among the major volcanic eruptions of the twentieth century. For several days, explosion followed explosion, expelling tons of debris into the atmosphere. Then on June 15, 1991, at 2:30 P.M., night descended. A gigantic ash plume more than 20 miles high rose into the sky. It fanned out to form a mushroom shape around 250 miles in diameter.

Fortunately, the people had been warned of the dangers they would face. During the weeks leading up to the eruption, videocassettes that volcanologists had supplied showed a similar eruption and the consequences it had produced. Thanks to this safety warning, the people living nearest the volcano realized they had to evacuate. They did, and — for now at least — many lives were saved.

Sulfur from Kawah Ijen, Island of Java

What is he doing, the man in this yellow world plunged in steam? He is working, but he's not a volcanologist. He's a miner who, along with many others, climbs down onto the crater floor each day to harvest sulfur.

Asia

It may look like a scene from a science-fiction movie. But to the men who come here, day after day, it is not play but hard, dangerous work. Kawah Ijen Volcano on the island of Java, in Indonesia, is peculiar in one important respect. The volcano releases large quantities of an acidic steam that crystallizes and hardens as it cools. And as it cools and hardens, sulfur forms. The steam gets its beautiful yellow color from the sulfur. Miners can then climb down into the crater and take the sulfur out. The miners' work is extremely difficult. First they must hack up the sulfur with blows from a crowbar. Then they load it into wicker baskets that they carry on their backs up to the crater's edge. From here, the sulfur is transported to a processing plant. But all day long, the workers breathe in the harmful gases, which burn their lungs. Sulfur, of course, is an important product. It is needed to make fertilizers. It is used in the oil industry and elsewhere, too. But it all starts here, with brave (and low-paid) workers going into steam-filled craters every day.

Puy de Dôme Volcano in Auvergne, France

The volcanoes in Auvergne, in central-eastern France, are round and green! But take care, for their history has probably not yet run its course. They are simply sleeping, for a period of time that can't be predicted. One day, they may wake up …

Europe

Not all volcanoes — as you can tell from this picture — billow with smoke or burst with flames. Some, quiet for centuries, lie like disk-shaped green fields. But remember, the Earth's center is never still. And where it broke through to leave its message of fire in the past — it may do so once again.

Recall that our planet's surface is composed of a number of plates. Volcanic activity normally occurs at the edges of these plates. Sometimes, though, in other places enormous updrafts of heat rise from the Earth's depths. We call these hot spots.

This is how the Auvergne volcanoes were born. A hot spot began by pushing outward. Then it broke through the Earth's crust, and magma spewed through the fissures it created. About 100 volcanoes formed, creating the chain of the Puys, in today's France. When one admires their rounded, lush green shapes, it is hard to believe that they once spit out fire. But our prehistoric ancestors saw them erupting. And we know that one day they will awaken again.